GIANT OCEAN ANIMALS

GREAT WHITE SHARK

Huge Hunter

BY EMMANUEL MARSHALL

Enslow PUBLISHING

Please visit our website, www.enslow.com. For a free color catalog of all our high-quality books, call toll free 1-800-398-2504 or fax 1-877-980-4454.

Library of Congress Cataloging-in-Publication Data
Names: Marshall, Emmanuel.
Title: Great white shark / Emmanuel Marshall.
Description: Buffalo, NY : Enslow Publishing, 2027. | Series: Giant ocean animals | Includes glossary and index.
Identifiers: ISBN 9781978550650 (pbk.) | ISBN 9781978550667 (library bound) | ISBN 9781978550674 (ebook)
Subjects: LCSH: White shark--Juvenile literature.
Classification: LCC QL638.95.L3 M377 2027 | DDC 597.33--dc23

Published in 2027 by
Enslow Publishing
2544 Clinton Street
Buffalo, NY 14224

Portions of this work were originally authored by Angela Lim and published as *Great White Sharks*. All new material in this edition was authored by Emmanuel Marshall.

Cover Designer: Joshua Olson
Interior Designer: Joshua Olson
Editor: Noah Riccardi

Photo Credits: Cover, p. 1 Sergey Uryadnikov/Shutterstock.com; pp. 4–5 Al Carrera/Shutterstock.com; pp. 6–7 Ramon Carretero/iStockphoto; pp. 8–9 Shane Myers Photography/Shutterstock.com; pp. 10–11 izanbar/iStockphoto; pp. 12–13 Jacques Star/Shutterstock.com; pp. 14–15 Jim Agronick/Shutterstock.com; pp. 16–17, 19, 29 Philip Thurston/iStockphoto; p. 18 USO/iStockphoto; pp. 20–21 webguzs/iStockphoto; pp. 22–23 slowmotiongli/Shutterstock.com; pp. 24–25 Okyela/Shutterstock.com; pp. 26–27 Catwalk Photos/Shutterstock.com.

Printed in China

CPSIA compliance information: Batch #QS27ENS For further information contact Enslow Publishing, at 1-800-398-2504.

TABLE OF CONTENTS

CHAPTER 1

FIERCE PREDATORS

Great white sharks are huge fish. They can grow 20 feet (6 m) long, though most are smaller. Great whites are known for being fierce **predators**.

Great whites may leap out of the water when they hunt.

Great white sharks mainly hunt seals. They may also eat turtles, squid, dolphins, or other sharks.

Each great white shark has about 300 teeth.

A great white shark's bite can **shatter** bone.

Great white may also act as scavengers. This means they may eat dead animals.

BIG FISH

The great white shark is one of the largest fish on Earth. Only two kinds of fish are bigger. They are the whale shark and basking shark.

One great white shark can eat around 11 tons (10 metric tons) of food each year.

CHAPTER 2

WHERE THEY LIVE

Great white sharks swim in oceans around the world. In fact, they have the widest **range** of any sea animal. They can be found near most continents.

Great whites can dive deep in cold ocean waters. They may also swim near shores.

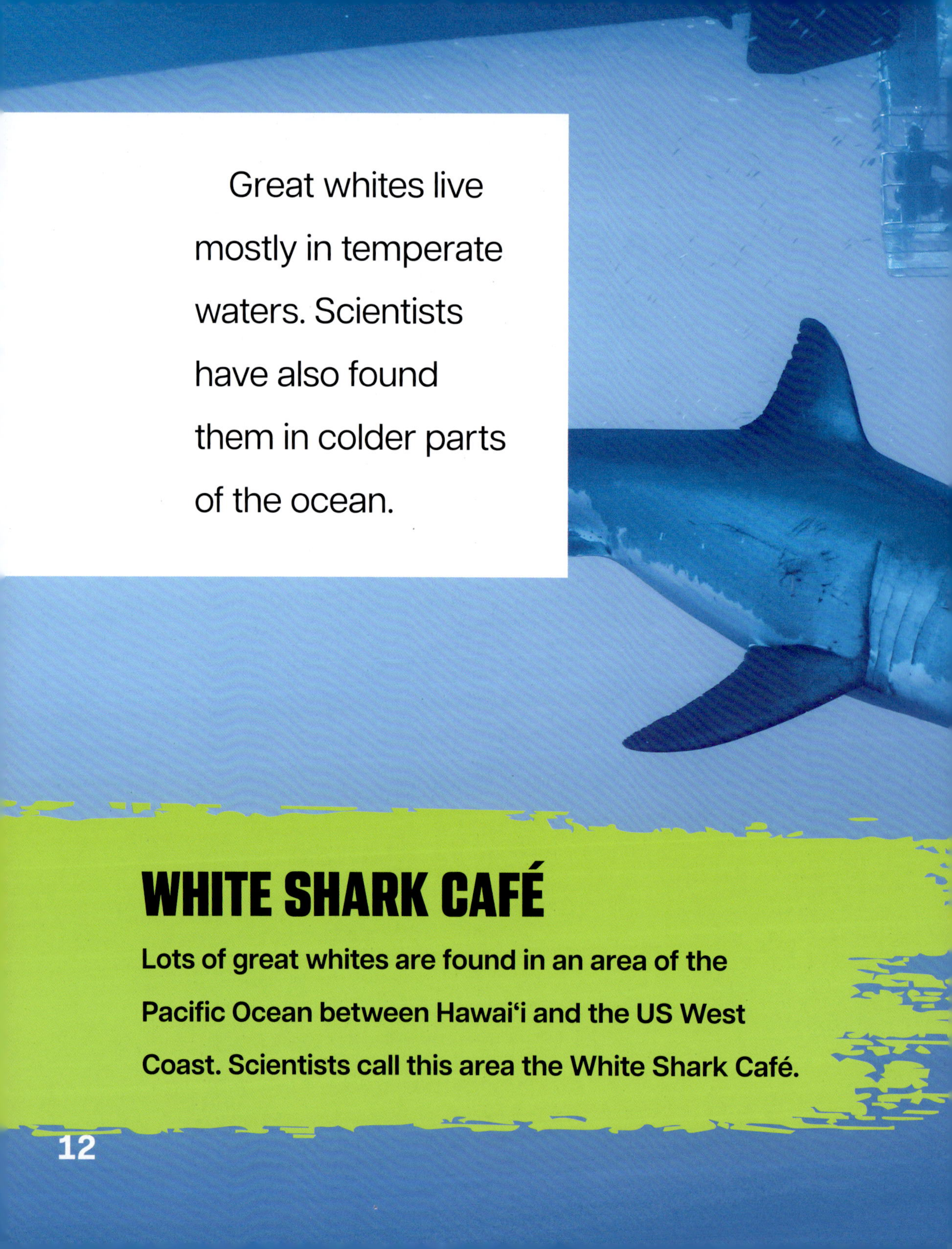

Great whites live mostly in temperate waters. Scientists have also found them in colder parts of the ocean.

WHITE SHARK CAFÉ

Lots of great whites are found in an area of the Pacific Ocean between Hawai‘i and the US West Coast. Scientists call this area the White Shark Café.

Diving in cages helps people get close to sharks safely.

Great white sharks sometimes swim to the ocean's surface to find food.

Sometimes great whites **migrate**. They swim great distances in the open ocean. Some great whites travel more than 1,550 miles (2,500 km).

Great whites can dive as deep as 3,940 feet (1,200 m).

CHAPTER 3

HOW THEY HUNT

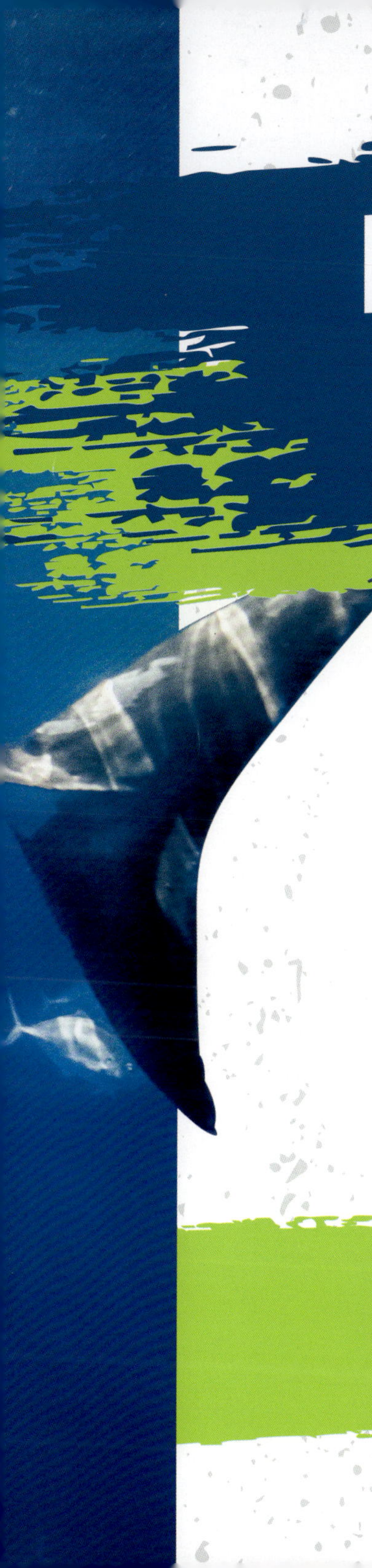

Several **adaptations** help great white sharks hunt. Most sharks are **cold-blooded**. But great whites can keep their bodies warm. That means they can swim in cold water. They can move fast, too.

Great white sharks are excellent hunters.

Great whites also have strong senses. They can smell blood. And they can sense the heartbeats of nearby animals.

A great white bursts out of the water to catch a seal.

Smelling blood helps great whites find food.

Great white sharks can smell one drop of blood in 25 gallons (95 L) of water.

The sharp teeth of a great white make it a dangerous hunter.

Finally, great whites are hard to spot. From below, their white bellies blend in with sunlight. From above, their gray bodies look like the rocky ocean floor.

SNEAK ATTACKS

Great whites often surprise their **prey**. The sharks watch for animals near the water's surface. They swim up and bite their prey from below.

CHAPTER 4

FACING DANGER

Great whites have few predators. Sometimes orcas kill and eat them. These huge dolphins attack young sharks. However, the main danger comes from humans.

Orcas flip sharks on their backs. That way, the sharks can't swim away.

Some people hunt great white sharks. Other people fish too much. That leaves less food for sharks. In the 1970s and 1980s, great whites were at risk of dying out. However, people took action.

Scientists believe that humans may hunt more than 100 million sharks per year.

Sharks rarely attack people.

Catching sharks for their fins is not allowed in US waters.

Great whites became a protected **species** in the United States and other countries. By the 2010s, their numbers had started to rise again. But some **populations** remain **endangered**.

HUMAN THREATS

People hunt great whites for many reasons. They use shark teeth to make necklaces. Shark fins are a popular dish in some countries.

TEST YOUR KNOWLEDGE

Take this quiz to test your knowledge.

1. Write a sentence describing adaptations that help a great white shark hunt.

2. Would you want to see a great white shark up close in a diving cage? Why or why not?

3. What animals eat great white sharks?

A. sea lions
B. orcas
C. seals

4. What do great white sharks use the scent of blood to do?

A. to hide from other fish
B. to reach the ocean floor
C. to find prey

5. What does **temperate** mean in this book?

*Great whites live mostly in **temperate** waters. Scientists have also found them in colder parts of the ocean.*

A. deep
B. warm
C. cold

6. What does **surface** mean in this book?

*The sharks watch for animals near the water's **surface**. They swim up and bite their prey from below.*

A. the top of the water
B. the very deep sea
C. a lot of dry land

Answers can be found on page 32.

GLOSSARY

adaptations
Abilities or features of animals that help them survive.

cold-blooded
Having a body temperature that matches the temperature of the surrounding water or air.

endangered
In danger of dying out forever.

migrate
To move from one part of the world to another.

populations
Groups of animals that live in particular places.

predators
Animals that hunt and eat other animals.

prey
An animal that is hunted and eaten by another animal.

range
The parts of the world where an animal can be found.

shatter
To break or destroy.

species
A group of animals or plants that are similar and can breed with one another.

FOR MORE INFORMATION

BOOKS

Griffin, Annabel. *Super Sharks*. Minneapolis, MN: Lerner Publications, 2023.

Ventura, Marne. *Sharks*. Minneapolis, MN: Abdo Publishing, 2023.

WEBSITES

Britannica Kids: White Shark

kids.britannica.com/kids/article/white-shark/602043

Learn more about great whites at this site.

National Geographic Kids: Surprising Sharks

kids.nationalgeographic.com/animals/fish/article/surprising-sharks

Learn about other kinds of sharks at this website.

Publisher's note to educators and parents: Our editors have carefully reviewed these websites to ensure that they are suitable for students. Many websites change frequently, however, and we cannot guarantee that a site's future contents will continue to meet our high standards of quality and educational value. Be advised that students should be closely supervised whenever they access the internet.

INDEX

Answer Key:
1. Answers will vary; 2. Answers will vary; 3. B; 4. C; 5. B; 6. A